Daily Bread

A daily devotional of
prayer and inspiration

CLIFF ROAD
BOOKS

**CLIFF ROAD
BOOKS**

Daily Bread

Scripture taken from the HOLY BIBLE: NEW INTERNATIONAL VERSION®. NIV®. Copyright © 1973, 1978, 1984 by International Bible Society.
Used by permission of The Zondervan Corporation.

The "NIV" and "New International Version" trademarks are registered in the United States Patent and Trademark Office by International Bible Society.
All rights reserved.

ISBN-13: 978-1-60261-338-6
ISBN-10: 1-60261-338-9

Cover design by Pat Covert

Printed in China

January 1

In the beginning was the Word, and the Word was with God, and the Word was God.

John 1:1

_____

_____

_____

_____

_____

_____

January 2

The LORD himself goes before you and will be with you; he will never leave you nor forsake you. Do not be afraid; do not be discouraged.

Deuteronomy 31:8

_____

_____

_____

_____

_____

January 3

❋

Lead me, O LORD, in your
righteousness because of my
enemies—make straight your way
before me.

Psalm 5:8

_____

_____

_____

_____

_____

_____

January 4

And I will do whatever you ask in my name, so that the Son may bring glory to the Father.

John 14:13

January 5

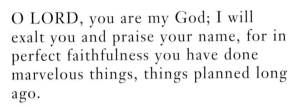

O LORD, you are my God; I will exalt you and praise your name, for in perfect faithfulness you have done marvelous things, things planned long ago.

Isaiah 25:1

_____

_____

_____

_____

_____

_____

January 6

The LORD is my strength and my song; he has become my salvation. He is my God, and I will praise him, my father's God, and I will exalt him.

Exodus 15:2

_____

_____

_____

_____

_____

_____

January 7

The fear of the LORD adds length to life, but the years of the wicked are cut short.

Proverbs 10:27

January 8

For just as through the disobedience of the one man the many were made sinners, so also through the obedience of the one man the many will be made righteous.

Romans 5:19

_____

_____

_____

_____

_____

_____

January 9

But the LORD is in his holy temple;
let all the earth be silent before him.

Habakkuk 2:20

January 10

When Jesus spoke again to the people, he said, "I am the light of the world. Whoever follows me will never walk in darkness, but will have the light of life."

John 8:12

_____

_____

_____

_____

_____

_____

January 11

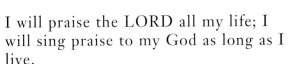

I will praise the LORD all my life; I will sing praise to my God as long as I live.

Psalm 146:2

_____

_____

_____

_____

_____

_____

January 12

Acknowledge and take to heart this day that the LORD is God in heaven above and on the earth below. There is no other.

Deuteronomy 4:39

_____

_____

_____

_____

_____

_____

January 13

O Sovereign LORD, you are God!
Your words are trustworthy, and you
have promised these good things to
your servant.

2 Samuel 7:28

_____

_____

_____

_____

_____

_____

January 14

❦

The fear of the LORD is the beginning of knowledge, but fools despise wisdom and discipline.

Proverbs 1:7

_____

_____

_____

_____

_____

_____

January 15

❦

He has showed you, O man, what is good. And what does the LORD require of you? To act justly and to love mercy and to walk humbly with your God.

Micah 6:8

_____

_____

_____

_____

_____

January 16

But the LORD Almighty will be exalted by his justice, and the holy God will show himself holy by his righteousness.

Isaiah 5:16

_____

_____

_____

_____

_____

_____

January 17

But if you do not forgive men their sins, your Father will not forgive your sins.

Matthew 6:15

_____

_____

_____

_____

_____

_____

January 18

Do to others as you would have them
do to you.

Luke 6:31

_____

_____

_____

_____

_____

_____

January 19

The earth is the LORD's, and everything in it, the world, and all who live in it; for he founded it upon the seas and established it upon the waters.

Psalm 24:1-2

_____

_____

_____

_____

_____

_____

January 20

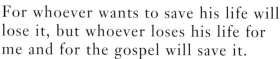

For whoever wants to save his life will lose it, but whoever loses his life for me and for the gospel will save it.

Mark 8:35

_____

_____

_____

_____

_____

_____

January 21

For God so loved the world that he gave his one and only Son, that whoever believes in him shall not perish but have eternal life.

John 3:16

_____

_____

_____

_____

_____

_____

January 22

And we know that in all things God works for the good of those who love him, who have been called according to his purpose.

Romans 8:28

_____

_____

_____

_____

_____

_____

January 23

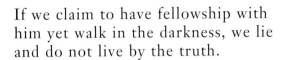

If we claim to have fellowship with
him yet walk in the darkness, we lie
and do not live by the truth.

1 John 1:6

January 24

❦

I am not ashamed of the gospel,
because it is the power of God for the
salvation of everyone who believes:
first for the Jew, then for the Gentile.

Romans 1:16

_____

_____

_____

_____

_____

_____

January 25

All the prophets testify about him that everyone who believes in him receives forgiveness of sins through his name.

Acts 10:43

January 26

Therefore do not worry about tomorrow, for tomorrow will worry about itself. Each day has enough trouble of its own.

Matthew 6:34

_____

_____

_____

_____

_____

_____

January 27

I have told you these things, so that in me you may have peace. In this world you will have trouble. But take heart! I have overcome the world.

John 16:33

_____

_____

_____

_____

_____

_____

January 28

❧

Who among the gods is like you, O
LORD? Who is like you—majestic in
holiness, awesome in glory, working
wonders?

Exodus 15:11

_____

_____

_____

_____

_____

_____

January 29

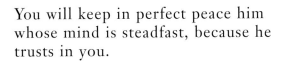

You will keep in perfect peace him whose mind is steadfast, because he trusts in you.

Isaiah 26:3

_____

_____

_____

_____

_____

_____

January 30

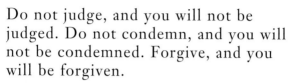

Do not judge, and you will not be judged. Do not condemn, and you will not be condemned. Forgive, and you will be forgiven.

Luke 6:37

_____

_____

_____

_____

_____

_____

January 31

Who is wise and understanding among you? Let him show it by his good life, by deeds done in the humility that comes from wisdom.

James 3:13

_____

_____

_____

_____

_____

_____

February 1

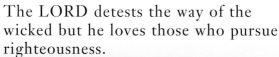

The LORD detests the way of the wicked but he loves those who pursue righteousness.

Proverbs 15:9

_____

_____

_____

_____

_____

_____

February 2

Now faith is being sure of what we hope for and certain of what we do not see.

Hebrews 11:1

February 3

Do not repay anyone evil for evil. Be careful to do what is right in the eyes of everybody.

Romans 12:17

_____

_____

_____

_____

_____

_____

February 4

Let the righteous rejoice in the
LORD and take refuge in him; let all
the upright in heart praise him!

Psalm 64:10

_____

_____

_____

_____

_____

_____

February 5

❦

Now this is eternal life: that they may know you, the only true God, and Jesus Christ, whom you have sent.

John 17:3

_____

_____

_____

_____

_____

_____

February 6

A gentle answer turns away wrath, but a harsh word stirs up anger.

Proverbs 15:1

_____

_____

_____

_____

_____

_____

February 7

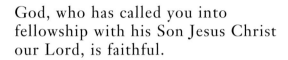

God, who has called you into fellowship with his Son Jesus Christ our Lord, is faithful.

1 Corinthians 1:9

February 8

But the fruit of the Spirit is love, joy, peace, patience, kindness, goodness, faithfulness, gentleness and self-control. Against such things there is no law.

Galatians 5:22-23

_____

_____

_____

_____

_____

_____

February 9

You are my lamp, O LORD; the
LORD turns my darkness into light.

2 Samuel 22:29

_____

_____

_____

_____

_____

_____

February 10

Jesus looked at them and said, "With man this is impossible, but not with God; all things are possible with God."

Mark 10:27

_____

_____

_____

_____

_____

_____

February 11

For it is by grace you have been saved, through faith—and this not from yourselves, it is the gift of God—not by works, so that no one can boast.

Ephesians 2:8-9

_____

_____

_____

_____

_____

_____

February 12

Do not judge, or you too will be judged. For in the same way you judge others, you will be judged, and with the measure you use, it will be measured to you.

Matthew 7:1-2

_____

_____

_____

_____

_____

_____

February 13

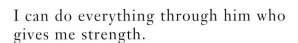

I can do everything through him who gives me strength.

Philippians 4:13

February 14

Dear children, let us not love with words or tongue but with actions and in truth.

1 John 3:18

_____

_____

_____

_____

_____

_____

February 15

❧

Therefore, I urge you, brothers, in
view of God's mercy, to offer your
bodies as living sacrifices, holy and
pleasing to God—this is your spiritual
act of worship.

Romans 12:1

_____

_____

_____

_____

_____

February 16

He is before all things, and in him all things hold together.

Colossians 1:17

_____

_____

_____

_____

_____

February 17

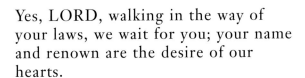

Yes, LORD, walking in the way of
your laws, we wait for you; your name
and renown are the desire of our
hearts.

Isaiah 26:8

_____

_____

_____

_____

_____

_____

February 18

Know that the LORD is God. It is he who made us, and we are his; we are his people, the sheep of his pasture.

Psalm 100:3

_____

_____

_____

_____

_____

February 19

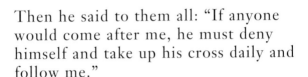

Then he said to them all: "If anyone would come after me, he must deny himself and take up his cross daily and follow me."

Luke 9:23

_____

_____

_____

_____

_____

_____

February 20

Make sure that nobody pays back
wrong for wrong, but always try to be
kind to each other and to everyone
else.

1 Thessalonians 5:15

_____

_____

_____

_____

_____

_____

February 21

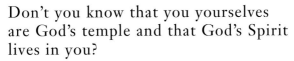

Don't you know that you yourselves
are God's temple and that God's Spirit
lives in you?

1 Corinthians 3:16

February 22

Live in harmony with one another. Do not be proud, but be willing to associate with people of low position. Do not be conceited.

Romans 12:16

_____

_____

_____

_____

_____

February 23

Trust in the LORD with all your heart
and lean not on your own
understanding; in all your ways
acknowledge him, and he will make
your paths straight.

Proverbs 3:5-6

_____

_____

_____

_____

_____

_____

February 24

The LORD is good to all; he has compassion on all he has made.

Psalm 145:9

_____

_____

_____

_____

_____

_____

February 25

Come near to God and he will come near to you. Wash your hands, you sinners, and purify your hearts, you double-minded.

James 4:8

_____

_____

_____

_____

_____

_____

February 26

Therefore, if anyone is in Christ, he is
a new creation; the old has gone, the
new has come!

2 Corinthians 5:17

_____

_____

_____

_____

_____

February 27

Jesus answered, "I am the way and the truth and the life. No one comes to the Father except through me."

John 14:6

_____

_____

_____

_____

_____

February 28

Humble yourselves, therefore, under God's mighty hand, that he may lift you up in due time. Cast all your anxiety on him because he cares for you.

1 Peter 5:6-7

_____

_____

_____

_____

_____

_____

February 29

❧

I will give you thanks, for you
answered me; you have become my
salvation.

Psalm 118:21

_____

_____

_____

_____

_____

_____

March 1

Observe the commands of the LORD
your God, walking in his ways and
revering him.

Deuteronomy 8:6

_____

_____

_____

_____

_____

_____

March 2

You are the light of the world. A city
on a hill cannot be hidden.

Matthew 5:14

March 3

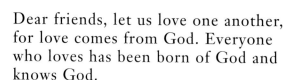

Dear friends, let us love one another, for love comes from God. Everyone who loves has been born of God and knows God.

1 John 4:7

_____

_____

_____

_____

_____

_____

March 4

LORD, you establish peace for us; all
that we have accomplished you have
done for us.

Isaiah 26:12

March 5

The LORD is my strength and my
shield; my heart trusts in him, and I
am helped. My heart leaps for joy and
I will give thanks to him in song.

Psalm 28:7

March 6

For the bread of God is he who comes down from heaven and gives life to the world.

John 6:33

March 7

If I give all I possess to the poor and surrender my body to the flames, but have not love, I gain nothing.

1 Corinthians 13:3

March 8

When you pass through the waters, I will be with you; and when you pass through the rivers, they will not sweep over you.

Isaiah 43:2a

_____

_____

_____

_____

_____

_____

March 9

It is for freedom that Christ has set us free. Stand firm, then, and do not let yourselves be burdened again by a yoke of slavery.

Galatians 5:1

_____

_____

_____

_____

_____

_____

March 10

If anyone acknowledges that Jesus is the Son of God, God lives in him and he in God.

1 John 4:15

_____

_____

_____

_____

_____

March 11

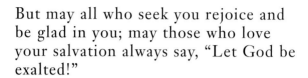

But may all who seek you rejoice and
be glad in you; may those who love
your salvation always say, "Let God be
exalted!"

Psalm 70:4

_____

_____

_____

_____

_____

_____

March 12

In my distress I called to the LORD; I called out to my God. From his temple he heard my voice; my cry came to his ears.

2 Samuel 22:7

_____

_____

_____

_____

_____

_____

March 13

May the LORD repay you for what you have done. May you be richly rewarded by the LORD, the God of Israel, under whose wings you have come to take refuge.

Ruth 2:12

March 14

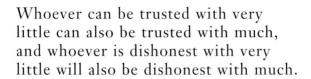

Whoever can be trusted with very
little can also be trusted with much,
and whoever is dishonest with very
little will also be dishonest with much.

Luke 16:10

March 15

Let us then approach the throne of grace with confidence, so that we may receive mercy and find grace to help us in our time of need.

Hebrews 4:16

_____

_____

_____

_____

_____

_____

March 16

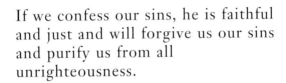

If we confess our sins, he is faithful
and just and will forgive us our sins
and purify us from all
unrighteousness.

1 John 1:9

_____

_____

_____

_____

_____

_____

March 17

Come, let us sing for joy to the LORD; let us shout aloud to the Rock of our salvation.

Psalm 95:1

_____

_____

_____

_____

_____

March 18

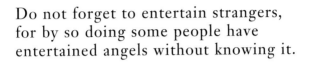

Do not forget to entertain strangers,
for by so doing some people have
entertained angels without knowing it.

Hebrews 13:2

March 19

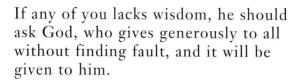

If any of you lacks wisdom, he should ask God, who gives generously to all without finding fault, and it will be given to him.

James 1:5

_____

_____

_____

_____

_____

_____

March 20

But the Lord is faithful, and he will strengthen and protect you from the evil one.

2 Thessalonians 3:3

_____

_____

_____

_____

_____

_____

March 21

But blessed is the man who trusts in
the LORD, whose confidence is in
him.

Jeremiah 17:7

_____

_____

_____

_____

_____

_____

March 22

Better a little with the fear of the LORD than great wealth with turmoil.

Proverbs 15:16

March 23

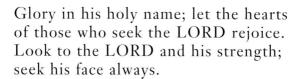

Glory in his holy name; let the hearts
of those who seek the LORD rejoice.
Look to the LORD and his strength;
seek his face always.

Psalm 105:3-4

_____

_____

_____

_____

_____

_____

March 24

Whoever serves me must follow me;
and where I am, my servant also will
be. My Father will honor the one who
serves me.

John 12:26

_____

_____

_____

_____

_____

_____

March 25

There are different kinds of gifts, but the same Spirit. There are different kinds of service, but the same Lord.

1 Corinthians 12:4-5

_____

_____

_____

_____

_____

_____

March 26

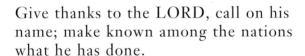

Give thanks to the LORD, call on his name; make known among the nations what he has done.

1 Chronicles 16:8

_____

_____

_____

_____

_____

_____

March 27

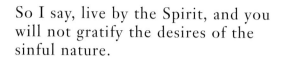

So I say, live by the Spirit, and you
will not gratify the desires of the
sinful nature.

Galatians 5:16

March 28

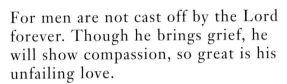

For men are not cast off by the Lord forever. Though he brings grief, he will show compassion, so great is his unfailing love.

Lamentations 3:31-32

_____

_____

_____

_____

_____

_____

March 29

For whoever does the will of my
Father in heaven is my brother and
sister and mother.

Matthew 12:50

_____

_____

_____

_____

_____

March 30

For God did not give us a spirit of
timidity, but a spirit of power, of love
and of self-discipline.

2 Timothy 1:7

_____

_____

_____

_____

_____

_____

March 31

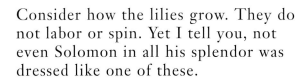

Consider how the lilies grow. They do not labor or spin. Yet I tell you, not even Solomon in all his splendor was dressed like one of these.

Luke 12:27

_____

_____

_____

_____

_____

_____

April 1

So do not fear, for I am with you; do not be dismayed, for I am your God. I will strengthen you and help you; I will uphold you with my righteous right hand.

Isaiah 41:10

_____

_____

_____

_____

_____

_____

April 2

In my Father's house are many rooms;
if it were not so, I would have told
you. I am going there to prepare a
place for you.

John 14:2

_____

_____

_____

_____

_____

_____

April 3

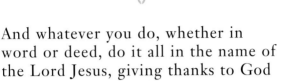

And whatever you do, whether in word or deed, do it all in the name of the Lord Jesus, giving thanks to God the Father through him.

Colossians 3:17

_____

_____

_____

_____

_____

_____

April 4

On the contrary, we speak as men approved by God to be entrusted with the gospel. We are not trying to please men but God, who tests our hearts.

1 Thessalonians 2:4

_____

_____

_____

_____

_____

_____

April 5

The LORD is near to all who call on him, to all who call on him in truth.

Psalm 145:18

April 6

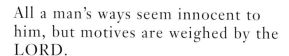

All a man's ways seem innocent to him, but motives are weighed by the LORD.

Proverbs 16:2

_____

_____

_____

_____

_____

_____

April 7

Consider it pure joy, my brothers, whenever you face trials of many kinds, because you know that the testing of your faith develops perseverance.

James 1:2-3

_____

_____

_____

_____

_____

April 8

In the same way, let your light shine before men, that they may see your good deeds and praise your Father in heaven.

Matthew 5:16

_____

_____

_____

_____

_____

_____

April 9

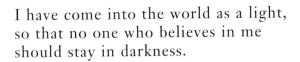

I have come into the world as a light,
so that no one who believes in me
should stay in darkness.

John 12:46

April 10

For whoever wants to save his life will lose it, but whoever loses his life for me will save it.

Luke 9:24

_____

_____

_____

_____

_____

_____

April 11

The LORD gives strength to his people; the LORD blesses his people with peace.

Psalm 29:11

_____

_____

_____

_____

_____

_____

April 12

Rather, worship the LORD your God; it is he who will deliver you from the hand of all your enemies.

2 Kings 17:39

_____

_____

_____

_____

_____

_____

April 13

The Spirit of God has made me; the
breath of the Almighty gives me life.

Job 33:4

April 14

❧

Be joyful always; pray continually;
give thanks in all circumstances, for
this is God's will for you in Christ
Jesus.

1 Thessalonians 5:16-18

_____

_____

_____

_____

_____

_____

April 15

Then Jesus said to them, "Give to
Caesar what is Caesar's and to God
what is God's." And they were amazed
at him.

Mark 12:17

_____

_____

_____

_____

_____

April 16

❧

But I tell you that men will have to give account on the day of judgment for every careless word they have spoken.

Matthew 12:36

April 17

To the LORD your God belong the heavens, even the highest heavens, the earth and everything in it.

Deuteronomy 10:14

April 18

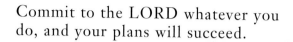

Commit to the LORD whatever you
do, and your plans will succeed.

Proverbs 16:3

April 19

I will come and proclaim your mighty acts, O Sovereign LORD; I will proclaim your righteousness, yours alone.

Psalm 71:16

_____

_____

_____

_____

_____

_____

April 20

Do not be afraid, little flock, for your Father has been pleased to give you the kingdom.

Luke 12:32

_____

_____

_____

_____

_____

April 21

❦

Choose my instruction instead of silver, knowledge rather than choice gold, for wisdom is more precious than rubies, and nothing you desire can compare with her.

Proverbs 8:10-11

_____

_____

_____

_____

_____

_____

April 22

There is no one holy like the LORD;
there is no one besides you; there is
no Rock like our God.

1 Samuel 2:2

_____

_____

_____

_____

_____

_____

April 23

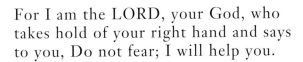

For I am the LORD, your God, who takes hold of your right hand and says to you, Do not fear; I will help you.

Isaiah 41:13

_____

_____

_____

_____

_____

_____

April 24

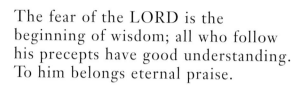

The fear of the LORD is the
beginning of wisdom; all who follow
his precepts have good understanding.
To him belongs eternal praise.

Psalm 111:10

_____

_____

_____

_____

_____

April 25

Heaven and earth will pass away, but my words will never pass away.

Matthew 24:35

April 26

Do not take revenge, my friends, but leave room for God's wrath, for it is written: "It is mine to avenge; I will repay," says the Lord.

Romans 12:19

_____

_____

_____

_____

_____

_____

April 27

How great you are, O Sovereign
LORD! There is no one like you, and
there is no God but you, as we have
heard with our own ears.

2 Samuel 7:22

April 28

Teach me to do your will, for you are
my God; may your good Spirit lead
me on level ground.

Psalm 143:10

April 29

❧

I tell you the truth, anyone who gives
you a cup of water in my name
because you belong to Christ will
certainly not lose his reward.

Mark 9:41

_____

_____

_____

_____

_____

_____

April 30

❧

When my life was ebbing away, I remembered you, LORD, and my prayer rose to you, to your holy temple.

Jonah 2:7

_____

_____

_____

_____

_____

_____

May 1

He who is not with me is against me,
and he who does not gather with me
scatters.

Matthew 12:30

_____

_____

_____

_____

_____

_____

May 2

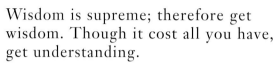

Wisdom is supreme; therefore get wisdom. Though it cost all you have, get understanding.

Proverbs 4:7

_____

_____

_____

_____

_____

_____

May 3

A new command I give you: Love one another. As I have loved you, so you must love one another.

John 13:34

_____

_____

_____

_____

_____

_____

May 4

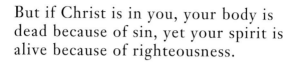

But if Christ is in you, your body is
dead because of sin, yet your spirit is
alive because of righteousness.

Romans 8:10

May 5

The God who made the world and everything in it is the Lord of heaven and earth and does not live in temples built by hands.

Acts 17:24

_____

_____

_____

_____

_____

_____

May 6

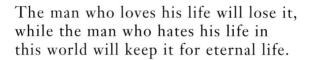

The man who loves his life will lose it,
while the man who hates his life in
this world will keep it for eternal life.

John 12:25

_____

_____

_____

_____

_____

_____

May 7

In the morning, O LORD, you hear my voice; in the morning I lay my requests before you and wait in expectation.

Psalm 5:3

_____

_____

_____

_____

_____

_____

May 8

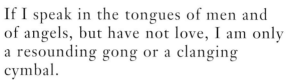

If I speak in the tongues of men and of angels, but have not love, I am only a resounding gong or a clanging cymbal.

1 Corinthians 13:1

_____

_____

_____

_____

_____

_____

May 9

Look at the nations and watch—and be utterly amazed. For I am going to do something in your days that you would not believe, even if you were told.

Habakkuk 1:5

_____

_____

_____

_____

_____

_____

May 10

If it is possible, as far as it depends on you, live at peace with everyone.

Romans 12:18

_____

_____

_____

_____

_____

_____

May 11

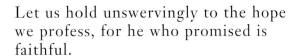

Let us hold unswervingly to the hope we profess, for he who promised is faithful.

Hebrews 10:23

May 12

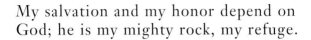

My salvation and my honor depend on
God; he is my mighty rock, my refuge.

Psalm 62:7

May 13

See, I am doing a new thing! Now it springs up; do you not perceive it? I am making a way in the desert and streams in the wasteland.

Isaiah 43:19

_____

_____

_____

_____

_____

_____

May 14

Blessed are the peacemakers, for they
will be called sons of God.

Matthew 5:9

_____

_____

_____

_____

_____

_____

May 15

As for God, his way is perfect; the word of the LORD is flawless. He is a shield for all who take refuge in him.

2 Samuel 22:31

May 16

❧

And anyone who does not carry his cross and follow me cannot be my disciple.

Luke 14:27

_____

_____

_____

_____

_____

_____

May 17

Do not be quick with your mouth, do not be hasty in your heart to utter anything before God. God is in heaven and you are on earth, so let your words be few.

Ecclesiastes 5:2

May 18

For whoever exalts himself will be
humbled, and whoever humbles
himself will be exalted.

Matthew 23:12

_____

_____

_____

_____

_____

May 19

❦

Jesus said to her, "I am the resurrection and the life. He who believes in me will live, even though he dies; and whoever lives and believes in me will never die."

John 11:25-26

_____

_____

_____

_____

_____

_____

May 20

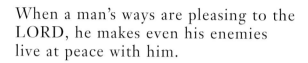

When a man's ways are pleasing to the
LORD, he makes even his enemies
live at peace with him.

Proverbs 16:7

_____

_____

_____

_____

_____

_____

May 21

Fear the LORD your God and serve him. Hold fast to him and take your oaths in his name.

Deuteronomy 10:20

_____

_____

_____

_____

_____

May 22

Therefore I tell you, whatever you ask for in prayer, believe that you have received it, and it will be yours.

Mark 11:24

_____

_____

_____

_____

_____

_____

May 23

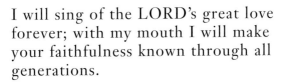

I will sing of the LORD's great love
forever; with my mouth I will make
your faithfulness known through all
generations.

Psalm 89:1

_____

_____

_____

_____

_____

May 24

❧

But God demonstrates his own love
for us in this: While we were still
sinners, Christ died for us.

Romans 5:8

_____

_____

_____

_____

_____

_____

May 25

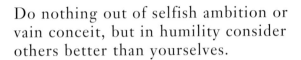

Do nothing out of selfish ambition or vain conceit, but in humility consider others better than yourselves.

Philippians 2:3

_____

_____

_____

_____

_____

_____

May 26

Every good and perfect gift is from above, coming down from the Father of the heavenly lights, who does not change like shifting shadows.

James 1:17

May 27

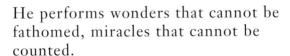

He performs wonders that cannot be fathomed, miracles that cannot be counted.

Job 5:9

_____

_____

_____

_____

_____

_____

May 28

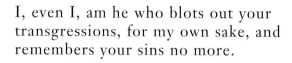

I, even I, am he who blots out your transgressions, for my own sake, and remembers your sins no more.

Isaiah 43:25

_____

_____

_____

_____

_____

_____

May 29

Sing to the LORD, praise his name;
proclaim his salvation day after day.

Psalm 96:2

_____

_____

_____

_____

_____

_____

May 30

If anyone has material possessions and sees his brother in need but has no pity on him, how can the love of God be in him?

1 John 3:17

_____

_____

_____

_____

_____

_____

May 31

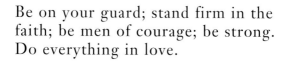

Be on your guard; stand firm in the faith; be men of courage; be strong. Do everything in love.

1 Corinthians 16:13-14

June 1

And do not forget to do good and to share with others, for with such sacrifices God is pleased.

Hebrews 13:16

_____

_____

_____

_____

_____

_____

June 2

Let us examine our ways and test them, and let us return to the LORD.

Lamentations 3:40

June 3

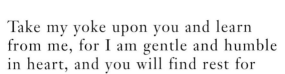

Take my yoke upon you and learn
from me, for I am gentle and humble
in heart, and you will find rest for
your souls.

Matthew 11:29

_____

_____

_____

_____

_____

_____

June 4

Whoever believes in me, as the
Scripture has said, streams of living
water will flow from within him.

John 7:38

_____

_____

_____

_____

_____

_____

June 5

Be kind and compassionate to one another, forgiving each other, just as in Christ God forgave you.

Ephesians 4:32

June 6

Praise the LORD. Sing to the LORD
a new song, his praise in the assembly
of the saints.

Psalm 149:1

_____

_____

_____

_____

_____

_____

June 7

Since, then, you have been raised with Christ, set your hearts on things above, where Christ is seated at the right hand of God.

Colossians 3:1

_____

_____

_____

_____

_____

_____

June 8

And now, dear children, continue in him, so that when he appears we may be confident and unashamed before him at his coming.

1 John 2:28

_____

_____

_____

_____

_____

_____

June 9

How much better to get wisdom than gold, to choose understanding rather than silver!

Proverbs 16:16

_____

_____

_____

_____

_____

_____

June 10

Sing to the LORD, all the earth;
proclaim his salvation day after day.

1 Chronicles 16:23

June 11

The end of a matter is better than its beginning, and patience is better than pride.

Ecclesiastes 7:8

_____

_____

_____

_____

_____

_____

June 12

❧

Keep your lives free from the love of money and be content with what you have, because God has said, "Never will I leave you; never will I forsake you."

Hebrews 13:5

_____

_____

_____

_____

_____

_____

June 13

This is what the LORD says—Israel's King and Redeemer, the LORD Almighty: I am the first and I am the last; apart from me there is no God.

Isaiah 44:6

_____

_____

_____

_____

_____

_____

June 14

Delight yourself in the LORD and he
will give you the desires of your heart.

Psalm 37:4

_____

_____

_____

_____

_____

_____

June 15

Be perfect, therefore, as your heavenly
Father is perfect.

Matthew 5:48

June 16

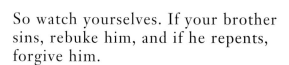

So watch yourselves. If your brother sins, rebuke him, and if he repents, forgive him.

Luke 17:3

_____

_____

_____

_____

_____

June 17

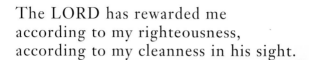

The LORD has rewarded me
according to my righteousness,
according to my cleanness in his sight.

2 Samuel 22:25

_____

_____

_____

_____

_____

_____

June 18

Instruct a wise man and he will be
wiser still; teach a righteous man and
he will add to his learning.

Proverbs 9:9

June 19

Through Jesus, therefore, let us continually offer to God a sacrifice of praise—the fruit of lips that confess his name.

Hebrews 13:15

_____

_____

_____

_____

_____

_____

June 20

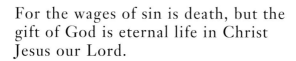

For the wages of sin is death, but the gift of God is eternal life in Christ Jesus our Lord.

Romans 6:23

_____

_____

_____

_____

_____

_____

June 21

❦

Put on the full armor of God so that you can take your stand against the devil's schemes.

Ephesians 6:11

_____

_____

_____

_____

_____

_____

June 22

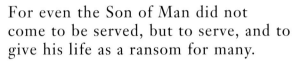

For even the Son of Man did not
come to be served, but to serve, and to
give his life as a ransom for many.

Mark 10:45

_____

_____

_____

_____

_____

_____

June 23

Better a patient man than a warrior, a man who controls his temper than one who takes a city.

Proverbs 16:32

_____

_____

_____

_____

_____

_____

June 24

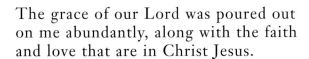

The grace of our Lord was poured out on me abundantly, along with the faith and love that are in Christ Jesus.

1 Timothy 1:14

_____

_____

_____

_____

_____

_____

June 25

I will give thanks to the LORD
because of his righteousness and will
sing praise to the name of the LORD
Most High.

Psalm 7:17

June 26

❦

In the same way, count yourselves
dead to sin but alive to God in Christ
Jesus.

Romans 6:11

_____

_____

_____

_____

_____

June 27

❧

Now then, my sons, listen to me;
blessed are those who keep my ways.
Listen to my instruction and be wise;
do not ignore it.

Proverbs 8:32-33

_____

_____

_____

_____

_____

_____

June 28

It is I who made the earth and created mankind upon it. My own hands stretched out the heavens; I marshaled their starry hosts.

Isaiah 45:12

_____

_____

_____

_____

_____

June 29

And if anyone gives even a cup of cold water to one of these little ones because he is my disciple, I tell you the truth, he will certainly not lose his reward.

Matthew 10:42

_____

_____

_____

_____

_____

_____

June 30

As for God, his way is perfect; the word of the LORD is flawless. He is a shield for all who take refuge in him.

Psalm 18:30

July 1

But as for me, I watch in hope for the LORD, I wait for God my Savior; my God will hear me.

Micah 7:7

_____

_____

_____

_____

_____

_____

July 2

He who pursues righteousness and
love finds life, prosperity and honor.

Proverbs 21:21

_____

_____

_____

_____

_____

_____

July 3

Until now you have not asked for
anything in my name. Ask and you
will receive, and your joy will be
complete.

John 16:24

_____

_____

_____

_____

_____

_____

July 4

Blessed is the nation whose God is the LORD, the people he chose for his inheritance.

Psalm 33:12

_____

_____

_____

_____

_____

_____

July 5

※

But be sure to fear the LORD and
serve him faithfully with all your
heart; consider what great things he
has done for you.

1 Samuel 12:24

_____

_____

_____

_____

_____

_____

July 6

I tell you the truth, he who believes
has everlasting life. I am the bread of
life.

John 6:47-48

July 7

And when you stand praying, if you
hold anything against anyone, forgive
him, so that your Father in heaven
may forgive you your sins.

Mark 11:25

_____

_____

_____

_____

_____

_____

July 8

He is your praise; he is your God, who performed for you those great and awesome wonders you saw with your own eyes.

Deuteronomy 10:21

_____

_____

_____

_____

_____

_____

July 9

I will extol the LORD at all times; his praise will always be on my lips.

Psalm 34:1

_____

_____

_____

_____

_____

July 10

There is no one like you, O LORD, and there is no God but you, as we have heard with our own ears.

1 Chronicles 17:20

July 11

The name of the LORD is a strong tower; the righteous run to it and are safe.

Proverbs 18:10

_____

_____

_____

_____

_____

_____

July 12

❧

Be careful not to do your 'acts of righteousness' before men, to be seen by them. If you do, you will have no reward from your Father in heaven.

Matthew 6:1

_____

_____

_____

_____

_____

_____

July 13

For sin shall not be your master,
because you are not under law, but
under grace.

Romans 6:14

July 14

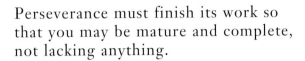

Perseverance must finish its work so
that you may be mature and complete,
not lacking anything.

James 1:4

_____

_____

_____

_____

_____

_____

July 15

❦

Because the Sovereign LORD helps
me, I will not be disgraced. Therefore
have I set my face like flint, and I
know I will not be put to shame.

Isaiah 50:7

July 16

Blessed are those who have learned to acclaim you, who walk in the light of your presence, O LORD.

Psalm 89:15

_____

_____

_____

_____

_____

_____

July 17

❧

My son, pay attention to my wisdom,
listen well to my words of insight, that
you may maintain discretion and your
lips may preserve knowledge.

Proverbs 5:1-2

_____

_____

_____

_____

_____

_____

July 18

❧

But if we walk in the light, as he is in the light, we have fellowship with one another, and the blood of Jesus, his Son, purifies us from all sin.

1 John 1:7

_____

_____

_____

_____

_____

_____

July 19

Whoever finds his life will lose it, and whoever loses his life for my sake will find it.

Matthew 10:39

_____

_____

_____

_____

_____

_____

July 20

❧

Greater love has no one than this, that
he lay down his life for his friends.
You are my friends if you do what I
command.

John 15:13-14

_____

_____

_____

_____

_____

_____

July 21

But now that you have been set free from sin and have become slaves to God, the benefit you reap leads to holiness, and the result is eternal life.

Romans 6:22

_____

_____

_____

_____

_____

_____

July 22

Let the heavens rejoice, let the earth be glad; let them say among the nations, "The LORD reigns!"

1 Chronicles 16:31

_____

_____

_____

_____

_____

_____

July 23

I love the LORD, for he heard my voice; he heard my cry for mercy.

Psalm 116:1

_____

_____

_____

_____

_____

_____

July 24

❦

Don't let anyone look down on you
because you are young, but set an
example for the believers in speech, in
life, in love, in faith and in purity.

1 Timothy 4:12

_____

_____

_____

_____

_____

_____

July 25

Love the LORD your God and keep his requirements, his decrees, his laws and his commands always.

Deuteronomy 11:1

_____

_____

_____

_____

_____

_____

July 26

Therefore do not let sin reign in your mortal body so that you obey its evil desires.

Romans 6:12

_____

_____

_____

_____

_____

_____

July 27

But your hearts must be fully committed to the LORD our God, to live by his decrees and obey his commands, as at this time.

1 Kings 8:61

_____

_____

_____

_____

_____

_____

July 28

The fear of the LORD is the beginning of wisdom, and knowledge of the Holy One is understanding.

Proverbs 9:10

July 29

※

For my Father's will is that everyone who looks to the Son and believes in him shall have eternal life, and I will raise him up at the last day.

John 6:40

_____

_____

_____

_____

_____

_____

July 30

❧

But I pray to you, O LORD, in the
time of your favor; in your great love,
O God, answer me with your sure
salvation.

Psalm 69:13

_____

_____

_____

_____

_____

_____

July 31

For if you forgive men when they sin against you, your heavenly Father will also forgive you.

Matthew 6:14

_____

_____

_____

_____

_____

_____

August 1

We know that we have passed from death to life, because we love our brothers. Anyone who does not love remains in death.

1 John 3:14

_____

_____

_____

_____

_____

_____

August 2

I the LORD search the heart and
examine the mind, to reward a man
according to his conduct, according to
what his deeds deserve.

Jeremiah 17:10

August 3

If you obey my commands, you will remain in my love, just as I have obeyed my Father's commands and remain in his love.

John 15:10

_____

_____

_____

_____

_____

_____

August 4

Dear friends, do not believe every
spirit, but test the spirits to see
whether they are from God, because
many false prophets have gone out
into the world.

1 John 4:1

_____

_____

_____

_____

_____

_____

August 5

But he was pierced for our transgressions, he was crushed for our iniquities; the punishment that brought us peace was upon him, and by his wounds we are healed.

Isaiah 53:5

August 6

Give thanks to the LORD, for he is good; his love endures forever.

Psalm 118:1

_____

_____

_____

_____

_____

_____

August 7

Whatever your hand finds to do, do it with all your might, for in the grave, where you are going, there is neither working nor planning nor knowledge nor wisdom.

Ecclesiastes 9:10

August 8

But I, with a song of thanksgiving, will sacrifice to you. What I have vowed I will make good. Salvation comes from the LORD.

Jonah 2:9

_____

_____

_____

_____

_____

_____

August 9

But seek first his kingdom and his righteousness, and all these things will be given to you as well.

Matthew 6:33

August 10

Unless the LORD builds the house,
its builders labor in vain. Unless the
LORD watches over the city, the
watchmen stand guard in vain.

Psalm 127:1

_____

_____

_____

_____

_____

_____

August 11

You came near when I called you, and you said, "Do not fear."

Lamentations 3:57

_____

_____

_____

_____

_____

August 12

I consider that our present sufferings
are not worth comparing with the
glory that will be revealed in us.

Romans 8:18

_____

_____

_____

_____

_____

_____

August 13

A man of many companions may come to ruin, but there is a friend who sticks closer than a brother.

Proverbs 18:24

August 14

❧

Therefore confess your sins to each other and pray for each other so that you may be healed. The prayer of a righteous man is powerful and effective.

James 5:16

_____

_____

_____

_____

_____

_____

August 15

This is how we know what love is:
Jesus Christ laid down his life for us.
And we ought to lay down our lives
for our brothers.

1 John 3:16

_____

_____

_____

_____

_____

_____

August 16

It is the LORD your God you must follow, and him you must revere. Keep his commands and obey him; serve him and hold fast to him.

Deuteronomy 13:4

August 17

And so we know and rely on the love
God has for us. God is love. Whoever
lives in love lives in God, and God in
him.

1 John 4:16

_____

_____

_____

_____

_____

_____

August 18

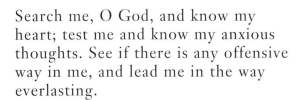

Search me, O God, and know my heart; test me and know my anxious thoughts. See if there is any offensive way in me, and lead me in the way everlasting.

Psalm 139:23-24

_____

_____

_____

_____

_____

_____

August 19

But the wisdom that comes from heaven is first of all pure; then peace-loving, considerate, submissive, full of mercy and good fruit, impartial and sincere.

James 3:17

_____

_____

_____

_____

_____

_____

August 20

Jesus Christ is the same yesterday and today and forever.

Hebrews 13:8

_____

_____

_____

_____

_____

_____

August 21

But since we belong to the day, let us be self-controlled, putting on faith and love as a breastplate, and the hope of salvation as a helmet.

1 Thessalonians 5:8

August 22

❧

Have I not commanded you? Be strong and courageous. Do not be terrified; do not be discouraged, for the LORD your God will be with you wherever you go.

Joshua 1:9

_____

_____

_____

_____

_____

_____

August 23

O LORD, our Lord, how majestic is
your name in all the earth! You have
set your glory above the heavens.

Psalm 8:1

_____

_____

_____

_____

_____

August 24

In your unfailing love you will lead the people you have redeemed. In your strength you will guide them to your holy dwelling.

Exodus 15:13

_____

_____

_____

_____

_____

_____

August 25

We all, like sheep, have gone astray,
each of us has turned to his own way;
and the LORD has laid on him the
iniquity of us all.

Isaiah 53:6

_____

_____

_____

_____

_____

_____

August 26

Therefore, get rid of all moral filth and the evil that is so prevalent and humbly accept the word planted in you, which can save you.

James 1:21

_____

_____

_____

_____

_____

_____

August 27

A man's wisdom gives him patience; it
is to his glory to overlook an offense.

Proverbs 19:11

August 28

But I call to God, and the LORD
saves me. Evening, morning and noon
I cry out in distress, and he hears my
voice.

Psalm 55:16-17

_____

_____

_____

_____

_____

_____

August 29

All that the Father gives me will come to me, and whoever comes to me I will never drive away.

John 6:37

August 30

That is why, for Christ's sake, I delight in weaknesses, in insults, in hardships, in persecutions, in difficulties. For when I am weak, then I am strong.

2 Corinthians 12:10

_____

_____

_____

_____

_____

_____

August 31

What goes into a man's mouth does not make him 'unclean,' but what comes out of his mouth, that is what makes him 'unclean.'

Matthew 15:11

_____

_____

_____

_____

_____

September 1

The LORD lives! Praise be to my
Rock! Exalted be God, the Rock, my
Savior!

2 Samuel 22:47

_____

_____

_____

_____

_____

_____

September 2

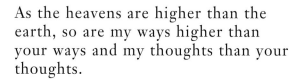

As the heavens are higher than the earth, so are my ways higher than your ways and my thoughts than your thoughts.

Isaiah 55:9

_____

_____

_____

_____

_____

_____

September 3

The LORD detests men of perverse heart but he delights in those whose ways are blameless.

Proverbs 11:20

September 4

How many are your works, O LORD!
In wisdom you made them all; the
earth is full of your creatures.

Psalm 104:24

_____

_____

_____

_____

_____

September 5

Whoever acknowledges me before
men, I will also acknowledge him
before my Father in heaven.

Matthew 10:32

_____

_____

_____

_____

_____

_____

September 6

Jesus answered, "It is written: 'Man does not live on bread alone.'"

Luke 4:4

September 7

For you did not receive a spirit that makes you a slave again to fear, but you received the Spirit of sonship. And by him we cry, "Abba, Father."

Romans 8:15

_____

_____

_____

_____

_____

_____

September 8

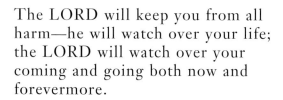

The LORD will keep you from all harm—he will watch over your life; the LORD will watch over your coming and going both now and forevermore.

Psalm 121:7-8

_____

_____

_____

_____

_____

_____

September 9

And the prayer offered in faith will make the sick person well; the Lord will raise him up. If he has sinned, he will be forgiven.

James 5:15

_____

_____

_____

_____

_____

_____

September 10

For the eyes of the LORD range throughout the earth to strengthen those whose hearts are fully committed to him.

2 Chronicles 16:9a

_____

_____

_____

_____

_____

_____

September 11

I will make you into a great nation
and I will bless you; I will make your
name great, and you will be a blessing.

Genesis 12:2

_____

_____

_____

_____

_____

September 12

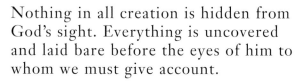

Nothing in all creation is hidden from God's sight. Everything is uncovered and laid bare before the eyes of him to whom we must give account.

Hebrews 4:13

_____

_____

_____

_____

_____

_____

September 13

But as for me, it is good to be near God. I have made the Sovereign LORD my refuge; I will tell of all your deeds.

Psalm 73:28

September 14

Blessed is the man whom God
corrects; so do not despise the
discipline of the Almighty.

Job 5:17

_____

_____

_____

_____

_____

_____

September 15

Do not say, "I'll pay you back for this wrong!" Wait for the LORD, and he will deliver you.

Proverbs 20:22

_____

_____

_____

_____

_____

_____

September 16

Therefore put on the full armor of God, so that when the day of evil comes, you may be able to stand your ground, and after you have done everything, to stand.

Ephesians 6:13

September 17

And he who searches our hearts knows the mind of the Spirit, because the Spirit intercedes for the saints in accordance with God's will.

Romans 8:27

_____

_____

_____

_____

_____

_____

September 18

Heal me, O LORD, and I will be
healed; save me and I will be saved,
for you are the one I praise.

Jeremiah 17:14

September 19

Those who obey his commands live in
him, and he in them. And this is how
we know that he lives in us: We know
it by the Spirit he gave us.

1 John 3:24

_____

_____

_____

_____

_____

_____

September 20

And now these three remain: faith, hope and love. But the greatest of these is love.

1 Corinthians 13:13

_____

_____

_____

_____

_____

_____

September 21

Sing to the LORD a new song, for he
has done marvelous things; his right
hand and his holy arm have worked
salvation for him.

Psalm 98:1

September 22

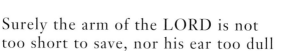

Surely the arm of the LORD is not
too short to save, nor his ear too dull
to hear.

Isaiah 59:1

September 23

It is my pleasure to tell you about the miraculous signs and wonders that the Most High God has performed for me.

Daniel 4:2

_____

_____

_____

_____

_____

_____

September 24

Let us not become weary in doing good, for at the proper time we will reap a harvest if we do not give up.

Galatians 6:9

September 25

I have no greater joy than to hear that my children are walking in the truth.

3 John 1:4

September 26

❦

Since we have these promises, dear friends, let us purify ourselves from everything that contaminates body and spirit, perfecting holiness out of reverence for God.

2 Corinthians 7:1

_____

_____

_____

_____

_____

_____

September 27

But let all who take refuge in you be glad; let them ever sing for joy. Spread your protection over them, that those who love your name may rejoice in you.

Psalm 5:11

_____

_____

_____

_____

_____

_____

September 28

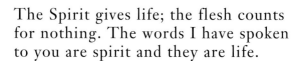

The Spirit gives life; the flesh counts
for nothing. The words I have spoken
to you are spirit and they are life.

John 6:63

_____

_____

_____

_____

_____

_____

September 29

❧

Again, I tell you that if two of you on earth agree about anything you ask for, it will be done for you by my Father in heaven.

Matthew 18:19

_____

_____

_____

_____

_____

_____

September 30

Then Peter began to speak: "I now realize how true it is that God does not show favoritism but accepts men from every nation who fear him and do what is right.

Acts 10:34-35

_____

_____

_____

_____

_____

_____

October 1

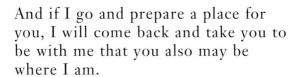

And if I go and prepare a place for you, I will come back and take you to be with me that you also may be where I am.

John 14:3

_____

_____

_____

_____

_____

_____

October 2

Bless those who persecute you; bless
and do not curse. Rejoice with those
who rejoice; mourn with those who
mourn.

Romans 12:14-15

October 3

The King will reply, "I tell you the truth, whatever you did for one of the least of these brothers of mine, you did for me."

Matthew 25:40

_____

_____

_____

_____

_____

_____

October 4

The LORD will establish you as his holy people, as he promised you on oath, if you keep the commands of the LORD your God and walk in his ways.

Deuteronomy 28:9

_____

_____

_____

_____

_____

_____

October 5

All a man's ways seem right to him,
but the LORD weighs the heart.

Proverbs 21:2

_____

_____

_____

_____

_____

_____

October 6

❦

The one who sows to please his sinful nature, from that nature will reap destruction; the one who sows to please the Spirit, from the Spirit will reap eternal life.

Galatians 6:8

_____

_____

_____

_____

_____

_____

October 7

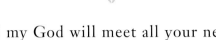

And my God will meet all your needs according to his glorious riches in Christ Jesus.

Philippians 4:19

_____

_____

_____

_____

_____

_____

October 8

If the LORD delights in a man's way,
he makes his steps firm; though he
stumble, he will not fall, for the
LORD upholds him with his hand.

Psalm 37:23-24

_____

_____

_____

_____

_____

_____

October 9

You, dear children, are from God and have overcome them, because the one who is in you is greater than the one who is in the world.

1 John 4:4

_____

_____

_____

_____

_____

_____

October 10

So then, those who suffer according to God's will should commit themselves to their faithful Creator and continue to do good.

1 Peter 4:19

_____

_____

_____

_____

_____

_____

October 11

The LORD does not look at the
things man looks at. Man looks at the
outward appearance, but the LORD
looks at the heart.

1 Samuel 16:7b

_____

_____

_____

_____

_____

_____

October 12

My soul yearns, even faints, for the courts of the LORD; my heart and my flesh cry out for the living God.

Psalm 84:2

_____

_____

_____

_____

_____

_____

October 13

Let your conversation be always full of grace, seasoned with salt, so that you may know how to answer everyone.

Colossians 4:6

_____

_____

_____

_____

_____

_____

October 14

And as for you, brothers, never tire of doing what is right.

2 Thessalonians 3:13

_____

_____

_____

_____

_____

_____

October 15

I am sending you out like sheep among wolves. Therefore be as shrewd as snakes and as innocent as doves.

Matthew 10:16

_____

_____

_____

_____

_____

_____

October 16

Yet, O LORD, you are our Father. We are the clay, you are the potter; we are all the work of your hand.

Isaiah 64:8

_____

_____

_____

_____

_____

_____

October 17

Praise the LORD, all his works
everywhere in his dominion. Praise
the LORD, O my soul.

Psalm 103:22

_____

_____

_____

_____

_____

_____

October 18

He who guards his lips guards his life, but he who speaks rashly will come to ruin.

Proverbs 13:3

October 19

Blessed is the man who perseveres under trial, because when he has stood the test, he will receive the crown of life that God has promised to those who love him.

James 1:12

October 20

❦

Now we know that if the earthly tent we live in is destroyed, we have a building from God, an eternal house in heaven, not built by human hands.

2 Corinthians 5:1

_____

_____

_____

_____

_____

_____

October 21

❧

Have no fear of sudden disaster or of
the ruin that overtakes the wicked, for
the LORD will be your confidence
and will keep your foot from being
snared.

Proverbs 3:25-26

October 22

Moreover, when God gives any man wealth and possessions, and enables him to enjoy them, to accept his lot and be happy in his work—this is a gift of God.

Ecclesiastes 5:19

_____

_____

_____

_____

_____

_____

October 23

But I tell you who hear me: Love your enemies, do good to those who hate you, bless those who curse you, pray for those who mistreat you.

Luke 6:27-28

_____

_____

_____

_____

_____

_____

October 24

I wait for your salvation, O LORD,
and I follow your commands. I obey
your statutes, for I love them greatly.

Psalm 119:166-167

_____

_____

_____

_____

_____

October 25

Get rid of all bitterness, rage and anger, brawling and slander, along with every form of malice.

Ephesians 4:31

_____

_____

_____

_____

_____

_____

October 26

A good name is more desirable than great riches; to be esteemed is better than silver or gold.

Proverbs 22:1

_____

_____

_____

_____

_____

October 27

Not everyone who says to me, 'Lord, Lord,' will enter the kingdom of heaven, but only he who does the will of my Father who is in heaven.

Matthew 7:21

_____

_____

_____

_____

_____

_____

October 28

Give thanks to the LORD, for he is good. His love endures forever.

Psalm 136:1

_____

_____

_____

_____

_____

_____

October 29

There is no fear in love. But perfect love drives out fear, because fear has to do with punishment. The one who fears is not made perfect in love.

1 John 4:18

_____

_____

_____

_____

_____

_____

October 30

Endure hardship as discipline; God is treating you as sons. For what son is not disciplined by his father?

Hebrews 12:7

_____

_____

_____

_____

_____

_____

October 31

Therefore do not be foolish, but understand what the Lord's will is.

Ephesians 5:17

_____

_____

_____

_____

_____

_____

November 1

A patient man has great understanding, but a quick-tempered man displays folly.

Proverbs 14:29

November 2

Since you are my rock and my
fortress, for the sake of your name
lead and guide me.

Psalm 31:3

November 3

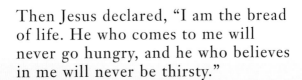

Then Jesus declared, "I am the bread of life. He who comes to me will never go hungry, and he who believes in me will never be thirsty."

John 6:35

_____

_____

_____

_____

_____

_____

November 4

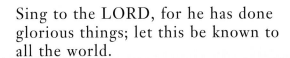

Sing to the LORD, for he has done glorious things; let this be known to all the world.

Isaiah 12:5

_____

_____

_____

_____

_____

_____

November 5

This is the victory that has overcome
the world, even our faith.

1 John 5:4

November 6

Sing to the LORD, you saints of his;
praise his holy name.

Psalm 30:4

November 7

If you believe, you will receive
whatever you ask for in prayer.

Matthew 21:22

November 8

Humility and the fear of the LORD
bring wealth and honor and life.

Proverbs 22:4

November 9

And God is able to make all grace abound to you, so that in all things at all times, having all that you need, you will abound in every good work.

2 Corinthians 9:8

_____

_____

_____

_____

_____

_____

November 10

We give thanks to you, O God, we give thanks, for your Name is near; men tell of your wonderful deeds.

Psalm 75:1

November 11

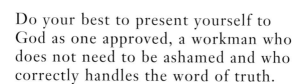

Do your best to present yourself to God as one approved, a workman who does not need to be ashamed and who correctly handles the word of truth.

2 Timothy 2:15

November 12

Now the Lord is the Spirit, and where the Spirit of the Lord is, there is freedom.

2 Corinthians 3:17

_____

_____

_____

_____

_____

_____

November 13

You give me your shield of victory;
you stoop down to make me great.

2 Samuel 22:36

_____

_____

_____

_____

_____

_____

November 14

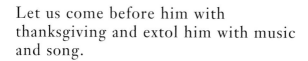

Let us come before him with thanksgiving and extol him with music and song.

Psalm 95:2

November 15

This is the confidence we have in approaching God: that if we ask anything according to his will, he hears us.

1 John 5:14

November 16

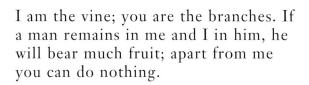

I am the vine; you are the branches. If a man remains in me and I in him, he will bear much fruit; apart from me you can do nothing.

John 15:5

_____

_____

_____

_____

_____

_____

November 17

When you have eaten and are satisfied, praise the LORD your God for the good land he has given you.

Deuteronomy 8:10

_____

_____

_____

_____

_____

November 18

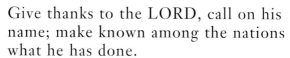

Give thanks to the LORD, call on his name; make known among the nations what he has done.

Psalm 105:1

_____

_____

_____

_____

_____

_____

November 19

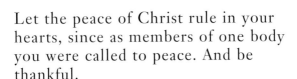

Let the peace of Christ rule in your hearts, since as members of one body you were called to peace. And be thankful.

Colossians 3:15

November 20

Do not boast about tomorrow, for you
do not know what a day may bring
forth.

Proverbs 27:1

_____

_____

_____

_____

_____

_____

November 21

When you ask, you do not receive,
because you ask with wrong motives,
that you may spend what you get on
your pleasures.

James 4:3

_____

_____

_____

_____

_____

_____

November 22

Enter his gates with thanksgiving and his courts with praise; give thanks to him and praise his name.

Psalm 100:4

November 23

And he has given us this command:
Whoever loves God must also love his
brother.

1 John 4:21

_____

_____

_____

_____

_____

_____

November 24

For every house is built by someone,
but God is the builder of everything.

Hebrews 3:4

November 25

❦

For the LORD God is a sun and
shield; the LORD bestows favor and
honor; no good thing does he
withhold from those whose walk is
blameless.

Psalm 84:11

_____

_____

_____

_____

_____

_____

November 26

Many are the plans in a man's heart,
but it is the LORD's purpose that
prevails.

Proverbs 19:21

_____

_____

_____

_____

_____

_____

November 27

Do not merely listen to the word, and so deceive yourselves. Do what it says.

James 1:22

_____

_____

_____

_____

_____

_____

November 28

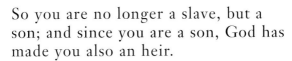

So you are no longer a slave, but a
son; and since you are a son, God has
made you also an heir.

Galatians 4:7

_____

_____

_____

_____

_____

_____

November 29

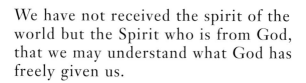

We have not received the spirit of the world but the Spirit who is from God, that we may understand what God has freely given us.

1 Corinthians 2:12

_____

_____

_____

_____

_____

_____

November 30

I have told you this so that my joy may be in you and that your joy may be complete.

John 15:11

_____

_____

_____

_____

_____

_____

December 1

A fool spurns his father's discipline,
but whoever heeds correction shows
prudence.

Proverbs 15:5

_____

_____

_____

_____

_____

_____

December 2

What good is it for a man to gain the whole world, yet forfeit his soul?

Mark 8:36

December 3

You may ask me for anything in my name, and I will do it.

John 14:14

_____

_____

_____

_____

_____

_____

December 4

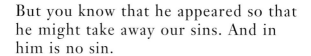

But you know that he appeared so that he might take away our sins. And in him is no sin.

1 John 3:5

_____

_____

_____

_____

_____

_____

December 5

For where two or three come together
in my name, there am I with them.

Matthew 18:20

_____

_____

_____

_____

_____

_____

December 6

I will praise God's name in song and glorify him with thanksgiving.

Psalm 69:30

December 7

Therefore, as we have opportunity, let
us do good to all people, especially to
those who belong to the family of
believers.

Galatians 6:10

_____

_____

_____

_____

_____

_____

December 8

For a man's ways are in full view of the LORD, and he examines all his paths.

Proverbs 5:21

December 9

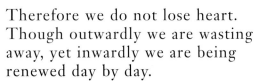

Therefore we do not lose heart.
Though outwardly we are wasting
away, yet inwardly we are being
renewed day by day.

2 Corinthians 4:16

_____

_____

_____

_____

_____

_____

December 10

Be not afraid, O land; be glad and
rejoice. Surely the LORD has done
great things.

Joel 2:21

_____

_____

_____

_____

_____

_____

December 11

The path of the righteous is level; O upright One, you make the way of the righteous smooth.

Isaiah 26:7

December 12

If you, then, though you are evil,
know how to give good gifts to your
children, how much more will your
Father in heaven give good gifts to
those who ask him!

Matthew 7:11

_____

_____

_____

_____

_____

December 13

Remain in me, and I will remain in you. No branch can bear fruit by itself; it must remain in the vine. Neither can you bear fruit unless you remain in me.

John 15:4

_____

_____

_____

_____

_____

_____

December 14

I will proclaim the name of the
LORD. Oh, praise the greatness of
our God!

Deuteronomy 32:3

_____

_____

_____

_____

_____

_____

December 15

For who is God besides the LORD?
And who is the Rock except our God?

2 Samuel 22:32

December 16

For the Son of Man is going to come
in his Father's glory with his angels,
and then he will reward each person
according to what he has done.

Matthew 16:27

December 17

If you remain in me and my words remain in you, ask whatever you wish, and it will be given you.

John 15:7

_____

_____

_____

_____

_____

_____

December 18

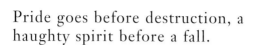

Pride goes before destruction, a
haughty spirit before a fall.

Proverbs 16:18

December 19

Your hands made me and formed me;
give me understanding to learn your
commands.

Psalm 119:73

December 20

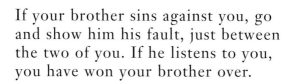

If your brother sins against you, go
and show him his fault, just between
the two of you. If he listens to you,
you have won your brother over.

Matthew 18:15

December 21

If anyone is ashamed of me and my words, the Son of Man will be ashamed of him when he comes in his glory and in the glory of the Father and of the holy angels.

Luke 9:26

_____

_____

_____

_____

_____

_____

December 22

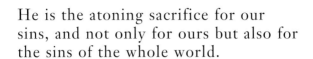

He is the atoning sacrifice for our
sins, and not only for ours but also for
the sins of the whole world.

1 John 2:2

December 23

Seek the LORD while he may be
found; call on him while he is near.

Isaiah 55:6

_____

_____

_____

_____

_____

December 24

May the words of my mouth and the
meditation of my heart be pleasing in
your sight, O LORD, my Rock and
my Redeemer.

Psalm 19:14

_____

_____

_____

_____

_____

_____

December 25

The Word became flesh and made his dwelling among us. We have seen his glory, the glory of the One and Only, who came from the Father, full of grace and truth.

John 1:14

_____

_____

_____

_____

_____

_____

December 26

Thanks be to God for his indescribable gift!

2 Corinthians 9:15

_____

_____

_____

_____

_____

_____

December 27

Ask and it will be given to you; seek and you will find; knock and the door will be opened to you.

Matthew 7:7

_____

_____

_____

_____

_____

_____

December 28

No, in all these things we are more than conquerors through him who loved us.

Romans 8:37

_____

_____

_____

_____

_____

_____

December 29

What you heard from me, keep as the pattern of sound teaching, with faith and love in Christ Jesus.

2 Timothy 1:13

_____

_____

_____

_____

_____

_____

December 30

This is how we know that we love the children of God: by loving God and carrying out his commands.

1 John 5:2

_____

_____

_____

_____

_____

_____

December 31

Peace I leave with you; my peace I give you. I do not give to you as the world gives. Do not let your hearts be troubled and do not be afraid.

John 14:27

_____

_____

_____

_____

_____

_____